RAND NATIONAL DEFENSE RESEARCH INSTITUTE

Advising the Command

Best Practices from the Special Operation's Advisory Experience in Afghanistan

Todd C. Helmus

Prepared for the Special Operations Joint Task Force–Afghanistan

For more information on this publication, visit www.rand.org/t/rr949

Library of Congress Cataloging-in-Publication Data
ISBN: 978-0-8330-8891-8

Published by the RAND Corporation, Santa Monica, Calif.
© Copyright 2015 RAND Corporation
RAND® is a registered trademark.

The RAND Corporation is a research organization that develops solutions to public policy challenges to help make communities throughout the world safer and more secure, healthier and more prosperous. RAND is nonprofit, nonpartisan, and committed to the public interest.

RAND's publications do not necessarily reflect the opinions of its research clients and sponsors.

Support RAND
Make a tax-deductible charitable contribution at
www.rand.org/giving/contribute

www.rand.org

Preface

The purpose of this report is to identify best practices in operational-level advising from the special operations advisory mission in Afghanistan. The report also identifies key recommendations that are intended to help address key challenges in operational-level partnering. Findings are drawn from an analysis of the Special Operations Advisory Groups (SOAGs), which are part of the NATO Special Operations Component Command–Afghanistan/Special Operations Joint Task Force–Afghanistan (NSOCC-A/SOJTF-A). SOAGs advise headquarter elements of the Afghan Special Security Forces.

This research was sponsored by NSOCC-A/SOJTF-A and conducted within the International Security and Defense Policy Center of the RAND National Defense Research Institute, a federally funded research and development center sponsored by the Office of the Secretary of Defense, the Joint Staff, the Unified Combatant Commands, the Navy, the Marine Corps, the defense agencies, and the defense Intelligence Community.

For more information on the International Security and Defense Policy Center, see http://www.rand.org/nsrd/ndri/centers/isdp.html or contact the director (contact information is provided on the web page).

Contents

Summary

This report presents the findings of in-depth interviews conducted with special operators advising headquarters elements of the Afghan Special Security Forces (ASSF). The research for this report was initially conducted to help enhance the capability of Special Operations Forces (SOF) advisory efforts and to help prepare incoming advisory staff. Hopefully, the report's enduring value will be to inform the practices of U.S. and allied advisors who will undertake an array of partner capacity-building initiatives at the operational or headquarters level.

Senior SOF commanders in Afghanistan created Special Operations Advisory Groups (SOAGs) to train, advise, and assist headquarter elements of the ASSF. SOAGs are small formations of advisors who operate under NATO Special Operations Component Command–Afghanistan/Special Operations Joint Task Force–Afghanistan (NSOCC-A/SOJTF-A). Each individual SOAG is aligned with a headquarters element of the ASSF, including General Command of Police Special Units (GCPSU), the Afghan Local Police (ALP), Commandos, Ktah Khas, and Special Mission Wing (SMW). There is also a SOAG that works at both the Ministries of Defense and Interior and is referred to as the Ministry Advisory Group Special Operations Forces Liaison Element (MAG SOFLE).

To conduct this study, RAND conducted interviews with staff representing SOAGs for the GCPSU, ALP, Commandos, Ktah Khas, SMW, and the MAG SOFLE. Interviews focused on a limited set of topics with cross-SOAG applicability. Accordingly, findings are presented for the topics of rapport building, the advising engagement, integration, sustainability, pre-deployment training, and continuity of operations.

Rapport Building. A strong rapport between advisor and counterpart can enhance information sharing, increase the likelihood that advice will be accepted, and reduce coalition force risk. Short tour lengths and limited engagement opportunities make rapport building difficult, so advisors must proactively build relationships with Afghan counterparts. Language/cultural sensitivity skills and proximity to partner offices can expedite the rapport-building process. Nontransactional relationships are especially crucial and are cultivated through personal conversations and shared meals.

The Advising Engagement. Advising host-nation counterparts is a complex and nuanced task. There is a natural tendency for advisors to offer advice and solutions to their host-nation counterparts. But this advice can suffer from an overly Western perspective, fail to instill local buy-in, and represents a lost opportunity to develop host-nation problem-solving skills. The alternative is to advise with carefully calibrated questions. Such questions should solicit and capitalize on the goals of the host-nation forces, help local officers think through problem sets, weigh pros and cons of various courses of action, and craft host-nation-centric solutions. As one advisor observed, "A better approach is to get to know your counterpart and ask him: 'What are your goals, what do you want to see with your division, where do you want to take your department?'"

Integration of Advisors. U.S. and coalition advisors must ensure proper integration and coordination across the advisory force. Advisors have often found that they need to "mentor the mentors" in order to avoid advisor fratricide and overcome logjams in the apparatus of the host nation's security. One SOAG for example, has built a "rolodex of advisors" to facilitate engagements. NSOCC-A has also hosted SOAG functional "shuras" for both intelligence and logistics, which help facilitate information sharing and problem solving. To integrate up, SOAGs worked with the MAG SOFLE. Ministry advisors, such as the MAG SOFLE, can at times help dislodge key roadblocks affecting individual operational-level advisors. Ministry advisors can also help advisors and key advisory commands, such as NSOCC-A, better understand and align their priorities with those of the ministries.

Integration of Host-Nation Forces. Advisors must also work to facilitate connections between their advisory counterparts and others within the host nation's security force apparatus. Building such connections can have a number of benefits, including increased intelligence sharing, improved sustainment processes, and enhanced command and control. At times, SOAGs facilitated relationships among key but reluctant Afghan partners by making introductions, arranging meetings, and refusing to play the intermediary role. Several SOAGs have fostered staff processes that connected disparate staff sections and enhanced staff synchronization. In Afghanistan, joint coordination and integration of the Afghan National Security Forces, which include ASSF, was a particular challenge. To help overcome this, some SOAGs sought to work with tactical units to build joint relationships and promote joint exercises, with the hope that such experiences might "bubble up" to operational-level commands.

Sustainability. Appropriate advising practices can facilitate host-nation decisionmaking, ownership, problem-solving skills, and other capabilities critical to sustainability. SOAGs employed a variety of practices to this end. One SOAG, for example, has fostered forums that help integrate operations and intelligence. Another approach was to simplify partner-unit operations and equipment requirements—e.g., several SOAGs purposefully eliminated overly complex and expensive weapons from Afghan formations. One challenge confronting SOAGs, and surely other advisory units, is the continued provision of key enablers (air, intelligence, logistics, etc.) to host-nation units, as such provisions can foster dependency and short-circuit partner-unit problem-solving. To this end, it was recommended that NSOCC-A gradually wean ASSF units from coalition-provided enablers that will soon disappear.

Pre-Deployment Training. Advisors require substantive training in language and cultural skills, coalition force structure, partner-nation governing institutions, command and control, and logistics processes. It is also critical that advisors learn how to advise. Among SOAG advisors, Afghanistan-Pakistan (AFPAK) Hands and Ministry of Defense Advisors received the most systematic training and individual augmentees (IAs) received the least. NSOCC-A (or other relevant field commands) may wish to develop a regularly held block training event that trains advisory skills as well as language/culture and other educational requirements. IAs could attend this were they to receive advance notification of deployment. Downrange Officer Professional Development seminars should also be considered. As a long-term solution, we recommend that the Department of Defense consider reinstituting the six-week Vietnam-era Military Assistance Training and Advisor course in an effort to more thoroughly inculcate advisory skills within the U.S. military.

Continuity of Operations. Effective continuity means that new staff build on previous advisor practices and relationships, avoid "reinventing the wheel," and understand past successes and failures. Recommendations for enhancing staff continuity include (1) increasing tour lengths for key advisory positions (Director, J2, J3, and J4); (2) ensuring advance notification for deployments, thus allowing incoming staff time to prepare and make advance connections with field units; (3) properly organizing and maintaining key files on computer portals; (4) requiring outgoing personnel to create continuity books; and (5) harnessing experienced staff who can mentor continuity within the advisory unit. Ultimately, implementation of these or other continuity practices requires the active engagement of commanders. Such commanders should develop standard operating procedures for continuity and ensure that such standards are followed across the force.

Acknowledgments

I would like to thank the staff of each of the individual Special Operations Advisory Groups who participated in this study. It is their observations and wisdom that make up the abundance of this report. I would also like to thank the NSOCC-A's Commander's Initiative Group for supporting this effort, as well as several individuals who provided early reviews and critiques of manuscripts: Brigadier General (U.S. Army) Christopher Burns, Lieutenant Colonel (U.S. Army) Chris Hensley, Dr. Negeen Pegahi, and Dr. Daniel Egel. Colonel (U.S. Army, retired) Joseph Felter and Susan Everingham provided formal and critical reviews of the final report. I am indebted to each of these individuals for their insights. Any errors are my sole responsibility.

CHAPTER ONE

Introduction

U.S. efforts to build the capacity of and advise Afghan security forces have been a lynchpin of U.S. engagement efforts in Afghanistan. Capacity building has also been fundamental to other U.S. missions abroad, from Iraq and the Philippines to varied countries in the African continent and elsewhere. The advisory mission is particularly important for U.S. Special Operations Forces (SOF) who have worldwide commitments to training both foreign conventional and special operations units. Given the importance of this mission set, it is critical that the U.S. policymakers, operators, and coalition partners learn from recent training efforts in Afghanistan.

A training model that may prove particularly valuable for study is the Special Operations Advisory Group (SOAG) developed by the NATO Special Operations Component Command–Afghanistan/ Special Operations Joint Task Force–Afghanistan (NSOCC-A/ SOJTF-A). After years of focused train, advise, and assist operations at the tactical level, the command created SOAGs in 2013 to serve as its primary platform to advise the headquarters capacity of the Afghan Special Security Forces (ASSF).[1] SOAGs specifically work to build multidimensional operational and institutional capacities in ASSF headquarters elements that will enable the units to function independently of direct International Security Assistance Force (ISAF) sup-

---

[1] For a critical examination of SOF partnering at the tactical level, please see Austin Long, Todd C. Helmus, S. Rebecca Zimmerman, Christopher M. Schnaubelt, and Peter Chalk, *Building Special Operations Partnerships in Afghanistan and Beyond: Challenges and Best Practices from Afghanistan, Iraq, and Colombia*, Santa Monica, Calif.: RAND Corporation, forthcoming.

port. Individual SOAGs are aligned across each of the ASSF headquarter elements, including the Afghan National Army Special Operations Command (ANASOC), the General Command of Police Special Units (GCPSU), the Afghan Local Police (ALP) headquarters, Special Mission Wing (SMW), and Ktah Khas. See Text Box 1.1 for a description of each of these SOAG elements and their partnered headquarters.

Text Box 1.1. Summary Description of SOAGs and Partnered ASSF Units

GCPSU SOAG. The GCPSU SOAG partners with the General Command of Police Special Units (GCPSU). The GCPSU is a major directorate in the Ministry of the Interior (MOI) that falls under the Deputy Minister for Security. It oversees the MOI's National Mission Units (NMUs) and Provincial Special Units (PSUs, previously known as Provincial Response Companies). The NMUs and the PSUs conduct high-risk arrest, counterterrorism, and counternarcotic missions. The NMUs include Afghan Territorial Force (ATF) 444, based in Helmand; Commando Force (CF) 333 in Logar; and Crisis Response Unit (CRU) 222 in Kabul. PSUs are arrayed across 33 Afghan provinces. They have a dedicated intelligence capability in the form of the Investigative Surveillance Unit, or ISU.

ANASOC SOAG. The ANASOC SOAG, previously known as the Commando SOAG, partners with the Afghan National Army Special Operations Command (ANASOC), which is a division-level formation in the Afghan National Army (ANA). ANASOC's primary tactical units are ten battalion-sized Commando units referred to as special operations kandaks (SOKs). Commandos are an elite light infantry force somewhat analogous to U.S. Army Rangers. The Commandos are designed to conduct specialized light infantry operations, including reconnaissance, direct action, and internal defense operations. Each SOK has three companies of ANA Commandos and one company of ANA Special Forces (ANASF). In addition to the SOKs, ANASOC has a military intelligence battalion, a support battalion, and a SOF School of Excellence. ANASOC has also established two special operations brigade (SOB) headquarters that will serve a command and control (C2) function for the individual SOK battalions.

ALP SOAG. The ALP SOAG oversees the development of the ALP and partners with the ALP Headquarters located within the MOI. The ALP serves as a local defense force that seeks to defend communities against insurgents and other illegally armed groups. At the time of this writing, there are more than 28,000 Afghan local policemen arrayed across 150 districts. The program originated as a major arm of U.S. Village Stability Operations (VSO), in which U.S. SOF teams embedded in local villages, recruited and trained ALP members, and promoted security, governance, and development initiatives. These SOF teams are increasingly lifting off the battlefield with responsibility for ALP oversight and management shifted to the MOI.

SMW SOAG. The SMW SOAG partners with the Afghan SMW. The SMW primarily conducts assault force insertion and intelligence, surveillance, and reconnaissance (ISR) aviation operations under day and night conditions. SMW aircraft include the MI-17, a medium twin-turbine transport helicopter, and the PC-12, a single-engine turboprop airplane. The SMW SOAG oversees development of the SMW and the distribution and procurement of aviation assets. The Embedded Training Team (ETT) is a subordinate element of the SOAG that trains, advises, and assists the SMW maintenance staff and aircrews.

Ktah Khas SOAG. The Ktah Khas is a battalion-level tier-one strike force unit overseen by the Ministry of Defense (MOD). The Ktah Khas SOAG helps advise battalion staff and oversees training of the unit's tactical formations.

MAG SOFLE. The MAG SOFLE is not a SOAG element per se but advises the MOD/MOI to ensure that NSOCC-A/SOJTF-A priorities are understood by Afghan National Security Forces (ANSF) senior leadership. It also facilitates synchronization/nesting with ministerial-level plans, orders, and priorities.

In seeking to enhance ASSF command and control (C2) capacity and promote the long-term sustainability of these forces, SOAGs perform a variety of functions. SOAG staffers advise Afghan staff officers and work carefully to understand and then inform counterparts of challenges confronting tactical formations. They help Afghan commanders build sustainable unit C2 processes, streamline logistics, and integrate operations and intelligence. In addition, SOAGs continue to oversee fielding of U.S. and NATO equipment and ensure stewardship of international assistance funds.

This report provides a look inside the SOAG mission in order to identify key challenges confronting headquarters-level advisor efforts and to identify best practices that may enhance partner capacity and sustainability. The goal is to inform both ongoing partnership operations in Afghanistan and to serve as a resource guide for future partner training missions beyond Afghanistan.

This analysis relies on more than 50 interviews conducted at the ANASOC, GCPSU, ALP, SMW, and Ktah Khas SOAGs, as well as the Ministry Advisory Group Special Operations Force Liaison Element (MAG SOFLE).[2] The vast majority of participants were officers between the grades of O-3 and O-6. Given the various units under study, the background of interviewed advisors was varied and included representatives of U.S. Special Forces, U.S. Navy SEALs, service personnel from allied forces, and others. In addition, interviews were supplemented with a limited survey of the literature on train, advise, and assist, as well as advisory and consulting industry best practices.

---

[2] Participants for this study were generally representative of personnel within the SOAGs. The SOAGs are directed by an officer of rank O-6 or O-5, with most of the functional advisors (for logistics, intelligence, operations, etc.) serving at the rank of O-4–O-5, with some SOAGs also employing O-3 advisors. Furthermore, given the variety of different SOAG units, interviewed participants came from a variety of different home-station units, including conventional army, U.S. Special Forces, U.S. Navy SEALs, and representatives of coalition forces, including the British, Norwegian, and Australian militaries. All participants were informed that they had the right to refuse participation in the study. Interviewed officers at the rank of O-5 and below and enlisted personnel were informed that interviews were non-attribution and thus the study would not pair participant names with comments. Select senior officers and interviews with academic experts were given the option to have comments either attributed or not attributed.

The topics addressed in this report include rapport building, the advising engagement, integration of SOF advisors, integration of ASSF, sustainability, pre-deployment training, and continuity of operations. While each SOAG confronts a unique range of problem sets, we chose these topics because they represent a limited set of topics that span the SOAG mission (each topic was addressed in multiple SOAG interviews) and are critical to the SOAG goals of enhanced C2 capacity and sustainability. Virtually any advisory unit must deal with the issues of rapport (the basic relationship between advisor and advisee) and the practice of offering advice and counsel (the advising engagement), so these were considered central to inclusion in this report. Furthermore, as the SOAGs represent an operational unit with a rotating staff, both pre-deployment training and continuity of operations were considered critical. Finally, NSOCC-A command has recently highlighted the importance of sustainability and integrating both coalition staff and disparate ASSF headquarters. Consequently these topics were included in this report.[3] The specific value of each of these topics is summarized in Table 1.1. This research does not address a number of other topics commonly addressed in doctrine, including advisor-advisee rank discrepancy, promoting battle command capabilities, operational processes, and international efforts to equip and sustain the ASSF.[4] These and many other issues are important to address but were beyond the scope of this study.

It is important to note that this study has several limitations. First, the author did not conduct interviews with representatives of the ANSF and so was not able to incorporate the Afghan perspective into the study's observations or conclusions. Such interviews were not included by design, given the limited time available for study interviews, but should be considered in future research. Second, given

---

[3] Of course, these topics should not be considered an exhaustive list of critical factors. Indeed, there are a variety of other relevant topics, including fielding of equipment and weapons, stewardship of U.S. assistance funds, C2 of tactical operations, and officer education and promotion. These topics are worth considering in future analyses of partnering best practices.

[4] Headquarters, Department of the Army, *Security Force Assistance*, FM 3-07.1, 2009.

Table 1.1. Rationale for Key Topics Studied in This Report

Topic	Rationale for Inclusion
1. Rapport	Rapport represents the basic relationship between the advisor and his counterpart and helps establish trust, promote information sharing, increase the likelihood that an advisor's advice will be accepted, and enhance individual force protection.
2. The advising engagement	The advice and counsel provided by advisors helps Afghan counterparts recognize key challenges and implement lasting solutions.
3. Integration of SOF advisors	With coalition advisors spread throughout Afghanistan's security force infrastructure, individual actions of advisors can ripple across formations in unexpected ways. It is thus important to facilitate proper communication and coordination across the advisor networks.
4. Integration of ASSF	Building effective working relationships and integration processes within and across Afghan headquarters elements helps these units solve problems, enhance coordination, and overcome sustainment challenges, such as logistics.
5. Sustainability	A self-sustaining Afghan security force is a clear coalition objective, as it helps pave the way for a successful coalition force departure from Afghanistan.
6. Pre-deployment training	Effective pre-deployment training is critical, as it provides individual advisors and SOAG staff the requisite skills to promote Afghan capacity.
7. Continuity of operations	With the incoming and outgoing churn of U.S. and allied staff, there is a risk that old lessons learned will be ignored, key relationships with Afghan staff interrupted, and effective policies forgotten.

the self-reporting inherent in the data collection for this analysis, it is impossible to discern whether the partnership practices identified in this report improved ASSF outcomes more so than any alternative practices. The practices cited in this report tended to be those that (a) sought to address the goals identified in Text Box 1.1 and (b) appeared to directly or indirectly result in the intended positive outcome, had substantiation from prior research on partnership or mentorship practices, or could be justified based on a broader and more logical consideration of the practice. However, such determinations, made by either interviewed participants or by the author, are inherently subjective. Finally, the SOAG mission is one of constant evolution. As SOAG officers work together with their host-nation counterparts, current capacity-building initiatives will take root and make way for new initiatives and expanded growth. The best practices identified here for ASSF capacity building represent a snapshot in time and will soon be surpassed by new initiatives. These reviewed practices should thus not be seen as proscribed initiatives but simply exemplars of coalition capacity-building initiatives at an early stage of operational-level capacity building.

CHAPTER TWO

Rapport

"Because of the hostile environment and the frequent turn-over of advisors, most counterparts were resistant . . . to an advisor's attempt to establish rapport. Without personal and institutional reasons to bond, and given the short-term focus of advisors serving brief assignments, establishing rapport was a topic much easier discussed than accomplished." [1]

Numerous individuals interviewed for this report spoke of the importance of rapport. Summarizing a common sentiment, one officer from SMW noted, "When you advise, your job is a lot more about relationships than anything else."[2] Another likewise noted that rapport "gets you in the door."[3] Rapport is critical to the advisory effort on several levels. Rapport builds trust that allows Afghan counterparts to share information and open up about problems affecting the command. As one officer observed, it allows them to "give you the bad news."[4] Furthermore, this trust will make counterparts more inclined to accept and follow recommendations.[5] Finally, it arguably offers force

[1] Robert D. Ramsey III, "Advising Indigenous Forces: American Advisors in Korea, Vietnam, and El Salvador," *Global War on Terrorism Occasional Paper 18*, Fort Leavenworth, Kan.: Combat Studies Institute Press, 2006.

[2] Interview with SMW SOAG and ETT staff, Kabul, Afghanistan, October 28 to November 1, 2013.

[3] Outstation comment during SOAG Best Practices study outbrief, November 26, 2013.

[4] Interviews with GCPSU SOAG staff, Kabul, Afghanistan, October 4 and 5, 2013.

[5] David H. Maister, Charles H. Green, and Robert M. Galford, *The Trusted Advisor*, New York: The Free Press, 2000.

protection value, as individual mentees will be more likely to share and respond to information concerning individual threats.

Rapport building, however, can be a challenge for operational-level advising. First, as discussed in Chapter Seven (in the "Selection of Advisors" text box"), rapport building often requires natural relationship-building skills, which may or may not be shared by all assigned to the advisor mission. In addition, the very nature of advising senior officers relegates advisory meetings to, at most, daily one-hour events. Furthermore, many advisors live and work in separate facilities and so must commute to advisory meetings, a process that, in an active warzone, consumes time and force protection manpower.[6] Importantly, numerous individuals interviewed for this study attested that it can take one to three months for an advisor to establish a meaningful and influential relationship with his Afghan counterpart.[7] This is particularly problematic for the many advisors who operate on short, six-month tour lengths. One advisor, citing an often observed "mentor fatigue" on the part of Afghans, observed, "There is reluctance on part of Afghans to really open up to you because they get tired [of the constant influx of new advisors]. A six-month [tour] becomes, if you are lucky, five months of a working relationship. Four months is effectively what we get."[8]

---

[6]   As subsequently noted, this separation of advisor and host-nation counterpart is not always the case with some SOAGs, including the SMW and Commando SOAG, which are located immediately adjacent to Afghan counterparts.

[7]   The assessment that it takes approximately three months to build effective rapport with a counterpart was mentioned independently across four separate interviews (Interviews with GCPSU SOAG staff, Kabul, Afghanistan, October 4 and 5, 2013; interviews with GCPSU SOAG and with ALP SOAG staff, Kabul, Afghanistan, October 8, 2013.). It was also cited in a Vietnam-era analysis of the advisory experience: "Because it takes several months for an advisor to work effectively with his counterpart, the possibility of extending the length of tours should be studied; the present six months for battalion and Special Forces advisors might well be stretched to nine months" (Gerald Cannon Hickey, *The American Military Advisor and His Foreign Counterpart: The Case of Vietnam*, Santa Monica, Calif.: RAND Corporation, RM-4482-ARPA, 1965). The topic is also addressed in a study examining advisory lessons learned in Korea, Vietnam, and El Salvador (Ramsey, 2006).

[8]   Interviews with GCPSU SOAG staff, Kabul, Afghanistan, October 4 and 5, 2013.

It is therefore critical that advisors proactively build relationships with their counterparts. Interviews suggest that, in addition to sufficiently long tour lengths, key rapport-building ingredients include language/cultural sensitivity, work proximity, and nontransactional relationships.

Language and Cultural Skills

Both language and cultural sensitivity skills were identified as crucial to rapport.[9] One advisor noted that even a simple repertoire of 50 basic Dari words can help. He argues that the effect on the relationship is "huge": "It shows interest [and] respect, [and] legitimizes [the Afghans as having a worthy] culture."[10] Another argues that language skills "help break the ice. It lends itself to a more cordial interaction with the Afghans. So you are not starting three steps behind but three steps ahead."[11] Cultural training has the same effect. For example, officers assigned to the Afghanistan-Pakistan (AFPAK) Hands program, which was created by the Department of Defense to develop U.S. military expertise in the region, receive extensive training in both culture and language, which several program officers report has enhanced their efforts to build rapport.[12] As one AFPAK Hand noted, "We know what

---

[9] Robert Ramsey noted in his 2006 study that

> Lacking language skills, advisors were basically deaf. They did not understand what was being said around them. In Korea, advisors were totally dependent on their ROKA [Republic of Korea Army] translators. In South Vietnam, even with some basic language training, advisors were heavily dependent on their RVNAF [Republic of Vietnam Armed Forces] translators. In El Salvador, where some language skill was required, few advisors were native speakers. Without language training, communication is impaired.

[10] Interviews with ALP SOAG staff, Kabul, Afghanistan, October 8, 2013.

[11] Interviews with ALP SOAG staff, Kabul, Afghanistan, October 8, 2013.

[12] The AFPAK Hands program seeks to create a cadre of military officers focused heavily on developing and maintaining expertise on those two countries. The goal of the program is that officers would enlist in the program for a four-year commitment, during which they would deploy twice to Afghanistan and in the intervening years serve on U.S.-based, Afghanistan-related positions such as the Joint Staff.

to say [and] what not to say to [Afghan] leaders. Little things like not denying chai when they offer it and not denying food when they offer it. Knowing how to be comfortable holding hands and [greeting with a kiss on the cheek], whatever is required to break that ice. . . . It will open up doors and have them listen to you."[13]

Proximity

Living and office proximity to counterparts is also important. Several SOAGs operate adjacent to or even amid Afghan counterparts. ANASOC SOAG resides on a hill just above the ANASOC headquarters. As a result, meetings are frequent and can be scheduled on an impromptu basis. The SMW and its SOAG go one step further and share the same office building. The SOAG reported that the close proximity facilitates numerous daily conversations. The SOAG's ETT, which oversees aircrew and maintenance training, previously worked in this office for several years. The team shared daily meals with their Afghan counterparts and established extremely productive relationships. To make room for the SOAG, the ETT recently relocated to the airfield (only several hundred yards away), but even this slight move has made such gatherings more rare.[14] In contrast, the staff at both the ALP and GCPSU SOAGs must drive to the offices of their counterparts, which are located in downtown Kabul. Such visits require scheduling and preparation and so naturally lack the spontaneity of engagements that other base locations afford. The travel to and from the Afghan headquarters also requires force protection for vehicle movements. This requirement is particularly burdensome for the ALP SOAG. The ALP SOAG is small in size relative to other SOAGs, and a simple drive to the ALP headquarters can require nearly half of the SOAG staffers.[15]

---

[13] Interviews with ANASOC SOAG staff, Kabul, Afghanistan, October 8 and 9, 2013.

[14] Interviews with SMW SOAG and ETT staff, Kabul, Afghanistan, October 28 to November 1, 2013. Several ETT staff lamented the degree to which this relocation has limited their engagement with Afghan counterparts.

[15] Interviews with ALP SOAG staff, Kabul, Afghanistan, October 8, 2013.

Text Box 2.1. Build Rapport on the Edges

Rapport building should extend to both security and support staff within an Afghan headquarters. As seen on a visit to an Afghan ministry, SOAG advisors paid close attention to building rapport with seemingly low-level staffers. They spent time with each individual guard that they passed, stopping to give an embrace and ask about family and the recent Eid holiday. They also built relationships with front office staff, as these individuals were often the ones who control appointments and access. Summarizing their approach, one officer recounted,

> We try to make every guard, every lower-level servant feel recognized and seen as a person, both as a human being and as a professional. By giving that recognition, we win him over and gain acceptance. We hope this gives us some protection, because in certain areas we feel the guards appreciate this.

SOAG advisors felt that such interactions produced multiple benefits, including enhanced force protection and greater access. They also recognized that the kind interactions echoed across the broader staff, who appreciate the respect afforded to the lower personnel.

Nontransactional Relationships

Finally, nontransactional relationships are especially crucial to rapport. Otherwise known as "hanging out," nontransactional relationships happen in a variety of different ways. Most commonly applied, building nontransactional relationships means engaging in small talk about families and other interests at the outset of an advisory meeting. As one SMW officer observed, "The more you get to know and sit and have tea, and talk about random things, it buys you credibility that you can use to help for other advising concepts."[16] The author observed a

---

[16] Interviews with SMW SOAG and ETT staff, Kabul, Afghanistan, October 28 to November 1, 2013.

Norwegian officer perform this task with immense grace. In visits with ministry officials, he actively and patiently listened to Afghans talk at length on topics of their own choosing and used a variety of open-ended questions to solicit information sharing and advance dialogue. Only after the Afghan counterparts exhausted their own line of conversation did he advance topics from his agenda.[17]

Shared meals are also important and provide a rare opportunity for social bonding. Norwegian officers who worked in the MAG SOFLE sought to socialize with MOI staff and officials in their spare time. They looked for opportunities to have lunch with Afghans and reportedly extended offers for dinner.[18] The SMW ETT cultivated extremely close relationships with their counterparts, in part by routinely eating with colleagues in the Afghan dining facility. They initiated the relationship by regularly inviting the Afghans to the U.S. dining hall, and soon the Afghans reciprocated the invitations. Explaining the rationale, one senior noncommissioned officer (SNCO) observed that Afghans (like in many other cultures) value shared meals: "It is family time, regardless of if you are family."[19]

Ultimately, building bonds in this way requires an investment of time. It means starting an advising session without a predetermined time-allotment or rigid schedule of tasks. Sometimes a counterpart will want to get straight into business, and other times they will talk family for 5–10 minutes. It also means an openness to routinely accepting invitations for lunch or tea, even when no discernible business is at hand.

---

[17] Interviews with MAG SOFLE staff, Kabul, Afghanistan, October 21 and November 21, 2013.

[18] Interviews with MAG SOFLE staff, Kabul, Afghanistan, October 21 and November 21, 2013. The practice is very much akin to that of Task Force (TF) 51, where Norwegian SOF operators eat daily meals with their Afghan colleagues in CRU 222. In fact, the Norwegian government allocates money to the tactical advisors so that they can buy lunch for the Afghan operators.

[19] Interviews with SMW SOAG and ETT staff, Kabul, Afghanistan, October 28 to November 1, 2013.

Tour Lengths

Tour lengths represent a critical challenge to SOAG advisor efforts. Tour lengths of SOAG staffers vary considerably, from four to 12 months duration. U.S. marines and airmen, as well as many NATO personnel, often serve six-month tours. As previously noted, it reportedly takes one to three months for advisors to establish trusting relationships with their counterparts, which significantly cuts into a shortened tour. The problem is compounded by a reported "mentor fatigue" whereby Afghans tire of the revolving door of advisors.[20] Longer tours, in the realm of nine to 12 months, could help alleviate this problem in the future. At a minimum, it may be wise to ensure that staff for key operational advisory positions (such as the director, J2, J3, and J4) serve yearlong tours.

Summary

The rapport between an advisor and his or her counterpart can offer a number of benefits, increasing the possibility that an advisor's advice will be acted upon and reducing the risk to coalition forces. Because short tour lengths and limited engagement opportunities make rapport building difficult, advisors must assiduously work to build relationships with their Afghan counterparts. They should also work to enhance language and cultural sensitivity skills and, where possible, work in close proximity to partner-unit offices. Nontransactional relationships are especially crucial, and advisors can cultivate these through sharing meals, conversations, and other social activities. Given the challenges posed specifically by tour lengths, it may be wise for tour lengths of key advisory positions be extended to yearlong tours.

---

[20] Interviews with GCPSU SOAG staff, Kabul, Afghanistan, October 4 and 5, 2013.

CHAPTER THREE

The Advising Engagement

"You are often far more influential when you ask questions than when you give answers."[1]

The heart of the SOAG mission is the one-on-one engagement between an advisor and his counterpart. It is here that the advisor works with his counterpart to identify key challenges confronting the counterpart's headquarters and facilitate workable and lasting solutions. Such engagements are complex and nuanced. Done right, the mentee feels free to share self-critical information, understands and is not threatened by the perspective of the advisor, and takes ownership of problems and solutions. Each of these outcomes is critical to enhancing partner-unit capacity (see the text box later in this chapter for a discussion on use of interpreters).

Some advisors reported that they are able to achieve success through a direct approach where they identify a problem and inform Afghan counterparts of the necessary solution but other advisors found this approach counterproductive. First, this direct approach can instill a natural resistance. An ALP SOAG staffer offers that Afghans "reject being told what to do."[2] This observation is echoed in numerous books on advising and coaching.[3] Second, such solutions risk being Western-centric and importantly fail to instill buy-in and ownership on the part of the host-nation counterpart. Echoing an oft-quoted sentiment, one

---

[1]   Marty Brounstein, *Coaching and Mentoring for Dummies: A Reference for the Rest of Us*, Hoboken, N.J.: Wiley Publishing, Inc., 2000.

[2]   Interviews with ALP SOAG staff, Kabul, Afghanistan, October 8, 2013.

[3]   Brounstein, 2000; Maister, Green, and Galford, 2000.

advisor noted, "It is easy to get Afghans to say yes, but it is hard to get them to have buy-in."[4]

The alternative is to help counterparts craft their own solutions. SOAG advisors offer a variety of solutions to promote this ownership, but central to the task is to use carefully calibrated questions that help host-nation partners think through problem sets, understand pros and cons of various courses of action, and craft local-centric solutions. Several approaches are discussed below.

Work Off of Host-Nation Counterpart Goals

Several advisors argue that the best approach is to solicit and work off of host-nation counterpart goals rather than the goals of coalition forces. In the case of Afghanistan, the coalition certainly has innumerable goals and objectives for improved ASSF capability. The key is understanding how these goals nest or fall in line with *Afghan* objectives. At base, working off of a counterpart's goals can improve buy-in and ownership and create a path of least resistance for securing improvements in headquarters functioning.[5] Observes one ANASOC SOAG officer, "A better approach is to get to know your counterpart and ask him, 'What are your goals, what do you want to see with your division, where do you want to take your department?'"[6] It is then the advisor's responsibility to help his counterpart deconstruct the goal into an achievable outcome and turn it into concrete steps that the mentee can then act upon.[7]

---

[4]   Interviews with SMW SOAG and ETT staff, Kabul, Afghanistan, October 28 to November 1, 2013.

[5]   As one ANASOC SOAG advisor observed, "It is not what you want, it is what the Afghans want. . . . It has to start with [an Afghan goal]. . . . [Otherwise] you are just setting yourself up for failure." Interviews with ANASOC SOAG staff, Kabul, Afghanistan, October 8 and 9, 2013.

[6]   Interviews with ANASOC SOAG staff, Kabul, Afghanistan, October 8 and 9, 2013.

[7]   This is an approach advocated by COL (P) Christopher Burns, a reserve officer who recently served as NSOCC-A's J7 director. As a civilian, COL (P) Burns works as a corporate coach for UBS, where he coaches UBS's top financial earners to improve performance and

To illustrate the point, a SOAG advisor asked his counterpart in the G3 how he could improve his tactical operations center (TOC). The Afghan responded that he needed a more literate staff. The advisor dug deeper to help deconstruct this goal, "Why do you need a more literate staff?" The answer: "Because I am really disorganized and not keeping up with reporting." The advisor could not magically procure literate staff and so helped explore other options for organizing the TOC. In the end, a revamped layout for the TOC was chosen: They rearranged communications equipment, moved the Afghan's office, and built a shelf for operational orders. The G3 representative achieved his goal, and the command benefited from improved communications and reporting. The advisor used the same process to motivate the officer to increase utilization of the Afghan National Tracking System (ANTS), which tracks movement and location of Afghan vehicles. The Afghan officer kept the system locked and unused in a closet, asserting that the locational data was secret and so must be kept out of reach. Understanding that the Afghan goal was secrecy, the advisor worked with his counterpart and helped him identify a solution whereby he kept the system in the closet but ran a cable to a TOC monitor that could be turned off when the TOC was not secured. As the advisor notes, "Now they use it regularly, they pull grids, they can at least battle watch." He concludes, "You have your objective, but where you hike the football needs to be from an Afghan objective."[8]

This process also affords a valuable lesson for broader U.S. development goals for host-nation SOF outfits such as the ASSF: Command goals should be nested within Afghan (or other partner-unit) priorities and interests.

---

enhance teamwork. Interview with COL (P) Christopher Burns, Kabul, Afghanistan, October 16, 2013.

[8]   Interview with anonymous SOAG staff, Kabul, Afghanistan, date withheld.

Use the Socratic Method

Another variation is the Socratic method, whereby the advisor uses a series of questions that help lead the counterpart to a mutually agreed-upon solution.[9] The training advisor at one SOAG used an approach like this to help his counterpart improve the unit's training curriculum. He reminded his colleague of a recently published United Nations Assistance Mission Afghanistan (UNAMA) report that criticized the unit for human rights violations. He could have directly insisted on more human rights training, but instead asked, "How do you think we can address those [concerns]?" The Afghan suggested increasing training from three to four weeks but offered that maybe they needed to add more firearms training. The advisor responded that that was a good idea, but asked about what could help address the UNAMA issues. The Afghan concluded that they needed more human rights training.[10] The advisor concluded, "We want to get buy-in from the Afghans, and the best way to do this is to ask appropriate questions that will help lead them to come up with the answers."[11]

Give Options; Let Afghans Own the Solution

There are of course times when advisors can provide recommendations to their host-nation counterparts. For example, it may not be uncommon for a mentee to seek a recommended course of action from the advisor. Rather than simply asserting a lone recommendation (which risks appearing as an implied task), an option is to work *with* the counterpart to develop a series of options and help them identify corresponding pros and cons of each option. If necessary, one can then carefully offer a recommended course of action and in the end reassure that the

---

[9]   For more information on this approach see Maister, Green, and Galford, 2000.

[10]   The goal of this approach is not necessarily to lead the advisor's counterpart to adopt a preconceived position held by the advisor. It may not even be necessary for the advisor to agree with the decision made by the counterpart. However, the advisor will ultimately have to weigh and help the counterpart carefully consider the decision's risks and benefits.

[11]   Interviews with SOAG staff, Kabul, Afghanistan, date withheld.

Text Box 3.1. Effectively Using Interpreters

Interpreters are a single point of failure for nearly all communications between coalition and Afghan personnel. The staff at the ALP and GCPSU SOAGs were keenly attuned to this fact and so took great care in how they worked with their interpreters. Rather than relegate interpreters to a segregated office space, the ALP SOAG gave its Category 2 interpreter (who has U.S. citizenship and a security clearance) a desk alongside the rest of the team and encouraged him to sit in on weekly meetings and briefings. The interpreter was treated the same as other members of the SOAG, a process that gave the interpreter enhanced ownership over his responsibilities. They also took pains to educate the interpreters on key tasks. At the GCPSU SOAG, the J4 was sure to brief their interpreter on all the key issues that were to be discussed in upcoming meetings. The ALP SOAG likewise explained "the context of everything we ask them to do." Observed one senior staffer, "I don't want [the interpreter] to be just a conduit for information. I want [him] to be a thinking conduit for information." Getting feedback from interpreters is another best practice. The ALP SOAG commander sought the interpreter's recommendation prior to engagements and afterward requested feedback to ensure that his interactions were culturally appropriate.

ultimate decision is his to make. The authors of a book on professional consulting entitled *The Trusted Advisor* argue that such an approach can "help the person feel that the solution was (to a large extent) his or her idea, or at the very least, his or her decision."[12] Observed an advisor at GCPSU, "For me, it is all about being a human being, talk to the other guy, make him understand I am not doing his job, but help him explore other options and solutions he has not been thinking about."[13]

---

[12] Maister, Green, and Galford, 2000.

[13] Interviews with GDPSU SOAG staff, Kabul, Afghanistan, October 4 and 5, 2013.

Of course a variety of other advising approaches exist, but a full examination of these tactics is beyond the scope of this study. As will be addressed in Chapter Seven, advisors would benefit enormously from pre-deployment training that provides a broad overview of influence and advising tactics and gives them the opportunity to practice such tactics in vignettes and role-playing scenarios.

Summary

When advisors give host-nation counterparts advice and solutions, there is a natural risk that that advice will be overly Western-centric, fail to garner local buy-in, and represent a lost opportunity to develop problem-solving skills. Instead, advisors should advise with carefully calibrated questions that solicit and capitalize on the host nation's goals, help partners think through problem sets, weigh pros and cons of various courses of action, and craft local-centric solutions.

CHAPTER FOUR

Integration of SOF Advisors

> "I have been impressed with [our] ability to reach out and touch
> [coalition personnel] across the enterprise. Everyone is eager to help with
> your issues or to help accomplish the mission. Rarely do you call someone
> and get a shoulder shrug or blow off."[1]

To successfully enhance host-nation capacity, operational advisors
often need to leverage a broader network of U.S. and NATO advisors.
In Afghanistan, coalition advisors have been spread throughout the
ANSF as well as the MOD and MOI. The actions of advisors serving at
various echelons of the Afghan chain of command can ripple through
the Afghan formations. Proper communication and coordination
across these advisor networks can thus greatly enhance unit capability
and forestall potential problems. Advisors also benefit when they can
share lessons learned. Such integration, however, has been challenged
by the sheer size of the coalition force, extensive time demands on
SOAGs that limit networking activities, and natural tendency to focus
"down and in" on a given headquarters element rather than focusing
"up and out" on the broader formation. Proper integration requires
that SOAGs develop connections across the coalition force, within
individual SOAGs, and up and down the advisor chain of command.

SOAG advisors have found that they often need to mentor other
advisors in order to avoid advisor fratricide (i.e., when advisors make
conflicting advice) and help overcome key issues confronting ASSF.
A GCPSU SOAG advisor recounted a story in which an MOI official
cancelled transportation for police recruits to the Special Police Train-

---

[1]   Interviews with SMW SOAG and ETT staff, Kabul, Afghanistan, October 28 to November 1, 2013.

ing Center on the advice of a coalition advisor who was unfamiliar with the GCPSU command. To fix the problem, the SOAG advisor had to mentor the coalition advisor of the MOI official.[2] Other advisors across the SOAGs were doing the same. Observed a Commando SOAG officer, "We are doing our KLEs [key leader engagements] and tying [ANASOC] mentors [together with other coalition] mentors." To assist in this effort, they have created a rolodex of advisors. "We asked who are the coalition counterparts for the Afghans from low to high. . . . . The first phase is to map the network [and] understand the Afghan systems. On the Afghan and coalition side, who is up and out [across the MOD that] we have to engage with?"[3]

Advisors must also collaborate in a horizontal fashion by connecting with other SOAGs. The NSOCC-A command assiduously worked to develop this collaboration by hosting a twice-weekly video teleconference (VTC) hosted by the NSOCC-A deputy commander charged with overseeing the SOAG mission. All of the command's SOAGs participated in this VTC, which helped to disseminate key SOAG priorities, operational challenges, and best practices. In addition, NSOCC-A has hosted several J4 "shuras" at which all the SOAG J4s gather to discuss key challenges and identify common solutions. The ALP J4 notes that such shuras are "Very valuable . . . it is almost mandatory, to give everyone the same cohesive situational awareness of logistics." He continues, "We all face the same problems, but we have different points of contact. At some point up the chain, those contacts merge to be the same guy."[4] NSOCC-A has also hosted an intelligence shura that brought together all the SOAG J2s and other advisors from the MOI's National Targeting Exploitation Center (NTEC; MOI's intelligence integration center) and MOD's National Military Intelligence Center (NMIC). Plans were in the works for follow-on events that would help ensure the intelligence advisor network stays connected. The challenge will be in ensuring that such efforts become institutionalized rather than driven ad-hoc by the initiative of staff. In addition, it is likely that

2   Interviews with GCPSU SOAG staff, Kabul, Afghanistan, October 4 and 5, 2013.

3   Interviews with ANASOC SOAG staff, Kabul, Afghanistan, October 8 and 9, 2013.

4   Interviews with ALP SOAG staff, Kabul, Afghanistan, October 8, 2013.

functional shuras for other key staff sections, such as operations and personnel, would be valuable as well.

Beyond working across coalition advisors, SOAG advisors have found they need to work on vertical integration, both down and into tactical elements and up to the ministries. Effective coordination with subordinate advisors helped the SOAGs understand key problems affecting tactical units. These problems could then be addressed at the partnered headquarters or raised to the ministry level as necessary. The ALP SOAG kept constant tabs through SOF teams partnered with ALP units, but obviously worried about maintaining situational awareness as these teams continued to lift off the battlefield.[5] Meanwhile, GCPSU SOAG relied on a network of liaison officers (LNOs) at ISAF SOF that are affiliated with ISAF SOF's subordinate task forces to keep abreast of emerging problems with tactical operations and logistics.[6]

The MAG SOFLE advises MOD/MOI institutions to ensure that its senior leaders understand NSOCC-A concerns and priorities. As such it has been a key conduit for SOAGs to address ministry-level policies that affect their partnered headquarters. The ANASOC SOAG had routine and weekly communications with the MAG SOFLE in order to raise issues and facilitate KLEs that helped "dislodge the roadblock[s]."[7] The ALP SOAG calls such connections "invaluable" and notes that the networking alone "is a great thing."[8]

Many KLEs that sought to prompt policy changes at the ministry level have remained unpersuasive. One potential factor in this has been a mismatch in priorities between coalition and Afghan leadership. To this end, another task of the MAG SOFLE has been to help the SOAGs and the broader NSOCC-A command better understand ministry priorities and perspectives.[9] Ideally, U.S. and allied commands

---

[5]   Interviews with ALP SOAG staff, Kabul, Afghanistan, October 8, 2013.

[6]   Interviews with GCPSU SOAG staff, Kabul, Afghanistan, October 4 and 5, 2013.

[7]   Interviews with ANASOC SOAG staff, Kabul, Afghanistan, October 8 and 9, 2013.

[8]   Interviews with ALP SOAG staff, Kabul, Afghanistan, October 8, 2013.

[9]   Interviews with MAG SOFLE staff, Kabul, Afghanistan, October 21 and November 21, 2013.

such as NSOCC-A would use feedback on the priorities of its partner forces and ministries to in turn shape its own goals and development priorities for those forces. Such efforts put all partners on the same page and allow partnering efforts to begin with early buy-in from partner forces.[10]

Summary

Coalition advisors have been spread throughout the ANSF, and the actions of these advisors have affected ASSF units for either the better or worse. Consequently, SOF advisors have worked to coordinate efforts across the advisory force. To this end, several potential best practices for operational-level partnering include mentoring the mentors to avoid advisor fratricide and overcome ASSF logjams, hosting functional "shuras" within the SOAGs to help enhance information sharing and best practices, and working with the coalition advisors at the ministries, who can address unit issues at the ministerial level. Such ministerial advisors can also help U.S. and coalition advisory commands better understand and improve synchronization with host-government priorities and objectives.

---

[10] Recent RAND research, which analyzed partner-capacity outcomes in 29 countries where the United States was engaged in building partner capacity, found in part that alignment of U.S. and partner-nation goals and interests is a significant determinant of partnership success (Christopher Paul, Colin P. Clarke, Beth Grill, Stephanie Young, Jennifer D. P. Moroney, Joe Hogler, and Christine Leah, *What Works Best in Building Partner Capacity and Under What Circumstances?* Santa Monica, Calif.: RAND Corporation, MG-1253/1-OSD, 2013). Other relevant RAND work on security cooperation and building partner capacity includes Jefferson P. Marquis, Jennifer D. P. Moroney, Justin Beck, Derek Eaton, Scott Hiromoto, David R. Howell, Janet Lewis, Charlotte Lynch, Michael J. Neumann, and Cathryn Quantic Thurston, *Developing an Army Strategy for Building Partner Capacity for Stability Operations*, Santa Monica, Calif.: RAND Corporation, MG-942-A, 2010; Jennifer D. P. Moroney, Adam Grissom, and Jefferson P. Marquis, *A Capabilities-Based Strategy for Army Security Cooperation*, Santa Monica, Calif.: RAND Corporation, MG-563-A, 2007; Jennifer D. P. Moroney, Celeste Gventer, Stephanie Pezard, and Laurence Smallman, *Lessons from U.S. Allies in Security Cooperation with Third Countries: The Cases of Australia, France, and the United Kingdom*, Santa Monica, Calif.: RAND Corporation, TR-972-AF, 2011.

CHAPTER FIVE

Integration of ASSF

Achieving an integrated ASSF is a key goal of NSOCC-A and will likely be a major goal of U.S. and coalition partnering efforts beyond Afghanistan. Developing effective working relationships and integration processes is critical to sharing intelligence, improving battlefield coordination, and addressing problems with logistics, to name but a few. Interpersonal differences and institutional stovepipes, however, can challenge coalition efforts to facilitate effective collaboration of individual host-nation officers and units. To address this common problem, SOAG advisors have worked to build relationships both within and across ASSF units.

Within-Unit Integration

First, SOF advisors have sought to build and promote relationships among key staff. In 2013, the coalition transferred responsibility for much of the ALP logistics supply over to the MOI. To help the ALP J4 take control over his own logistics supply, the SOAG J4, relying on his own advisor networks, took his counterpart to the MOI and introduced him to the director of ammunition and armament and to key personnel in the Afghan material management center. His goal was to "Help [the ALP J4] understand who [these persons were] and what [they] can do for him. . . . Then they swap phone numbers, and so next time there is an issue . . . he calls him."[1] Such relationship building is especially important when relationships among Afghan officers are strained.[2] Within one command, "resentment and animosity" characterized the relationship between two Afghan intelligence officers who worked in separate offices. The SOAG advisor consequently brought the officers together for regularly scheduled meetings in an effort to "get them to talk" and hopefully improve the quality of their relationship.[3]

Beyond fostering individual relationships, another approach is to develop unit integration processes. ANASOC SOAG, for example, has developed an Operations and Intelligence (O&I) forum within ANASOC. Like coalition-held O&Is, the forum helped the ANASOC command integrate intelligence into its operations cycle. It also served a forcing function to facilitate staff communications. Observed one U.S. officer, "This is a way to get G3 and G2 to talk. [The] G1, 4, and 6 will [also] come. They do not do a good job of cross-talking and sharing information. [It forces] them to communicate."[4] ANASOC SOAG has also been working to seed ANASOC LNOs throughout relevant MOD institutions, such as the NMIC, as well as the supply depots.[5]

---

[1]   Interviews with ALP SOAG staff, Kabul, Afghanistan, October 8, 2013. In another example, a Camp Commando advisor took the ANASOC public affairs officer (PAO) with him to visit the chief PAO officer at the MOD. The ANASOC PAO was reluctant to release information to the media, but the arranged meeting allowed the MOD officer to give formal guidance on press releases, which in turn enhanced the ANASOC PAO performance. Interviews with ANASOC SOAG staff, Kabul, Afghanistan, October 8 and 9, 2013.

[2]   Coalition mentors can easily use mentor networks to achieve ends that could otherwise be accomplished through Afghan connections. At times, coalition advisors will bypass organic Afghan processes—for example, passing formal Afghan logistics requests through advisor networks rather than require Afghans to submit the forms themselves. In other cases, Afghans seek out advisor assistance. In one instance, a corps commander was misusing a tactical ASSF unit. The ASSF commander was reluctant to engage the corps commander because of a soured relationship and so sought NSOCC-A engagement to fix the problem. The commander of NSOCC-A, however, demurred, noting that it was vital for the ASSF commander to work the issue "point to point." Anonymous interview, date and location withheld.

[3]   Anonymous interview, date and location withheld.

[4]   Interviews with ANASOC SOAG staff, Kabul, Afghanistan, October 8 and 9, 2013.

[5]   Interviews with ANASOC SOAG staff, Kabul, Afghanistan, October 8 and 9, 2013.

GCPSU SOAG, meanwhile, created regularly held GCPSU J4 shuras that brought together relevant logistics officers from across the GCPSU command architecture, including MOI, GCPSU headquarters, and subordinate NMUs and PSUs. According to the GCPSU J4,

> If you get GCPSU level and MOI and then tactical units [together, then] all three levels will understand the problems they are facing. They will talk it through and find solutions and break out of problems. Often I see that solutions coming from tactical level could be really good solutions to guys at higher levels. . . .[6]

Joint Coordination

Facilitating joint or interagency coordination, especially in Afghanistan, is a particular challenge. At the Afghan MOD and MOI level, joint integration has not been a priority, and so there has been "no forcing function to make people work together."[7] This lack of coordination has been especially prevalent in intelligence sharing, an area where effective coordination could yield significant benefits. For example, there has been a tendency for national-level intelligence organizations to view each other as threats rather than potential allies, and distrust between the institutions has run rampant. The NSOCC-A command sought to address this challenge through a number of steps, most notably by hosting a commander's dinner that included all of the commanders of the varying ASSF outfits and their senior advisors. The dinner was meant to enable the varying commanders to socialize and interact with one another as a first step in fostering coordination.

Beyond this, some additional successes have been noted in Afghanistan at the tactical level. Some Commando battalions or kandaks have coordinated intelligence sharing with ANA Corps, National Directorate of Security (NDS), and MOI elements, includung ALP and the Afghan Border Police (ABP). Special police units working

---

[6]   Interviews with GCPSU SOAG staff, Kabul, Afghanistan, October 4 and 5, 2013.

[7]   Anonymous interview, date and location withheld.

under the GCPSU have also shown impressive coordination efforts. At CF 333, the J3 advisor has helped connect the CF 333 J2 with NTEC, to help advise NTEC on target packages, and they have fostered routine meetings with Special Investigative Units (SIU), provincial NDS officials, and others.[8] There has also been nascent coordination for joint training. This was especially seen with the SMW, where various ASSF tactical units were eager to build relationships. The MOI special police units, including the Kabul-based CRU 222 and CF 333, have built excellent relationships with SMW and have had routine training events. In addition, advisors at ANASOC SOAG have just recently established a working relationship with SMW, fostered by a leadership shura that brought together SMW aviators, ANASOC officers, and 6th SOK. Even if host-nation senior leaders are reluctant to promote joint coordination, there may be value in facilitating tactical integration and building relationships that can eventually "bubble up."

Summary

In summary, helping to integrate host-nation officers across and within partnered SOF units can foster a number of benefits, including increased intelligence sharing, improved sustainment processes, and enhanced C2. To enhance integration within individual units, advisors have worked to introduce counterparts to key players in higher-echelon commands, help address strained relationships among key staff, and foster unit processes that promote integration. To enhance joint coordination, a goal that will often be challenged by deep institutional stovepipes, SOF advisors have worked to promote connections between various tactical units, with the goal of having those connections "bubble up" to the headquarters level.

---

[8]   Austin Long, Todd C. Helmus, Rebecca Zimmerman, Christopher Schnaubelt, and Peter Chalk, *Building Special Operations Partnerships in Afghanistan and Beyond: Challenges and Best Practices from Afghanistan, Iraq, and Colombia*, Santa Monica, Calif.: RAND Corporation, forthcoming; Jason Campbell, Matthew Thomeczek and Todd C. Helmus, "Best Practices for Building SOF Partnership Capacity—Intelligence Highlights," NSOCC-A Commander's Initiative Group paper, September 24, 2013.

CHAPTER SIX

Sustainability

"This has to be Afghan-led, we are forcing the process. [We are] making sure all ISU [Investigative Surveillance Unit] reports go to NTEC. All the information is fed [in] to the Afghan system to get them to work and produce targets to get guys out on the ground to do arrests. This is working."[1]

"We have showed them enough and it's time to start coaching on the sidelines. They need to stand on their two feet and do it on their own." [2]

Building a self-sustaining partner security force is obviously a quintessential goal for nearly any command engaged in host-nation capacity building. The same is true of NSOCC-A's partnership with ASSF. Sustainability is a key goal that undergirds many of this report's best practices. Some activities of advisors, however, address sustainability more directly. These efforts were incredibly varied, with some advisors focusing on simplifying Afghan operations and logistics requirements, promoting effective unit processes, and weaning Afghans from coalition enablers that will soon disappear.

One approach to sustainment is to simplify. Several SOAG advisors spoke of efforts to simplify Afghan operations and logistics requirements by easing back on planned weapon systems for tactical elements. For example, the SMW SOAG cancelled plans for the MI-17 aircraft to carry electrically driven mini- or Gatling guns. They reasoned that the mini-gun weight displacement would significantly decrease aircraft

---

[1] Interviews with GCPSU SOAG staff, Kabul, Afghanistan, October 4 and 5, 2013.

[2] Anonymous interview, date and location withheld.

passenger capacity, be overly complicated to operate, and pose a huge burden on the logistics system, as it would be the only mini-gun in the Afghan arsenal. The SMW SOAG commander was likewise reluctant to purchase expensive navigation gear for newly arrived PC-12 fixed wing aircraft, as "paper maps" will do.[3] Another SOAG was seeking to eliminate a light artillery element and other complex weapon systems from its tactical formations. As one officer noted, "When you burden leaders, we complicate his solution to a problem." When asked for a principle to guide such acquisitions, he noted that it was best to "establish baseline effectiveness before you increase effectiveness" with equipment and special tactics.[4] Another potential rule of thumb is to pursue acquisitions and promote operational tactics that can reasonably be sustained after coalition forces draw down.[5] Regardless, advisors should routinely look for opportunities to simplify acquisition and logistics requirements as well as operational tactics, techniques, and procedures.[6]

Promoting sustainable unit process mechanisms is also critical. Unit process mechanisms form the basic building blocks of ongoing staff integration and problem solving. GCPSU SOAG, for example, has been working to improve intelligence operations integration within the GDPSU headquarters. The group has helped construct a robust targeting process for the NMUs by feeding collected intelligence reports from the GCPSU's Investigative Surveillance Unit to the MOI's NTEC, which can in turn develop warrant and targeting packets for the NMUs to act upon. This is in contrast to other coalition SOF efforts that feed U.S. and coalition intelligence directly to Afghan operational

---

[3]   Interview with SMW SOAG and ETT staff, Kabul, Afghanistan, October 28 to November 1, 2013.

[4]   Anonymous interview, date and location withheld.

[5]   See discussion on sustainability in Long et al., forthcoming.

[6]   These observations are reinforced by Christopher Paul and colleagues at RAND, who in their study on building partner capacity outcomes in 29 countries demonstrated that one of the key determinants of success was the United States building on existing baseline partner-nation capabilities, without providing more sophisticated equipment, assistance, or training than partner-nation forces are able to absorb. Paul et al., 2013.

units or action targets in a more unilateral fashion. Observed one officer, "What we should be doing is supporting the Afghan system, that means using NTEC and NDS to task national mission units to do ops [rather than action targets more directly]."[7] The GCPSU SOAG has also worked to build what it called a "bespoke" logistics system. Once equipment arrives at regional logistics centers, the SOAG notifies the GCPSU J4, who then goes directly to the logistics center to pick up the supplies. It is an unorthodox approach, but one that helps limit theft and unnecessary delays in supply.[8] The ANASOC SOAG has also implemented a number of process-oriented development programs for ANASOC. The O&I forums previously referenced are one such example, as they seek to engrain a focus on intelligence-driven operations within the Afghan command. The SOAG has also developed staff exercises in which ANASOC officers practice mission planning. The group is also working to improve the command's message traffic, a step that requires developing standard operating procedures throughout the ANASOC and subordinate formations.[9]

Finally, a number of advisors argued that it is critical to wean host-nation partner units from coalition enablers that will eventually disappear. This has been a critical issue in Afghanistan, as there were numerous examples of coalition assistance enabling Afghan operations, including providing supplies to Afghan units directly, transporting Afghan recruits to training centers, and expediting logistics requests by passing them through advisor networks. Several interview respondents noted that such enabling can hinder the development of Afghan processes. Observed one NSOCC-A officer, "We should be letting them fail and learn from it and have ownership. . . . So we go out and get ammo and solve their problem. You [created] a solution for today but never built a thinking process."[10] Another officer noted, "Because they know we are supporting [them], what happens to human beings

7   Interviews with GCPSU SOAG staff, Kabul, Afghanistan, October 4 and 5, 2013.

8   Interviews with GCPSU SOAG staff, Kabul, Afghanistan, October 4 and 5, 2013.

9   Interviews with ANASOC SOAG staff, Kabul, Afghanistan, October 8 and 9, 2013.

10   Anonymous interview, date and location withheld.

if they know you are a backup? There will be a change in reality."[11] These and other officers argue that there may be a tendency for Afghan commanders to rest on the laurels of U.S. and coalition assistance. Instead, the officers argue it may be best to allow some Afghan systems to fail in a noncatastrophic manner (e.g., non-life-threatening failures, such that new recruits fail to arrive at training centers, or operational units fail to receive ammunition and other supplies, thus limiting the ability to conduct routine operations) if it helps Afghan commanders take ultimate responsibility and initiative. To address this challenge, it will be important to increasingly wean ASSF units of enablers rather than continue to provide such assistance until doing so is ultimately impossible.[12]

Summary

SOAGs employ a variety of practices to enhance partner headquarter sustainability, including simplifying operations and logistics requirements to promote effective unit processes. To further enhance partner sustainability, advisors should work to gradually wean host-nation SOF units from coalition-provided enablers that will inevitably disappear.

---

[11]   Anonymous interview, date and location withheld.

[12]   In the meantime, one officer argued that one must push Afghan systems to "vulnerability," by holding off on enablers until the last moment. The example here is the need for the MOI to distribute winter uniforms to the ALP. The ALP SOAG will not let the MOI fail in the mission, and so if necessary will push the uniforms using coalition assets. However, the SOAG is placing constant pressure on the MOI to use its own distribution channels. Outstation comment during SOAG Best Practices study outbrief, November 26, 2013.

CHAPTER SEVEN

Pre-Deployment Training

"We put [in] a bad, . . . inappropriately equipped mentor, the Afghans will know [it] in a heartbeat. [The Afghans] will be culturally sensitive and superficially compliant."[1]

Effective training is critical. Most advisors enter Afghanistan with deep knowledge of their occupational specialties, but this knowledge alone is insufficient, as effective advising requires a host of new tools and capabilities.[2] For example, advisory missions in Afghanistan (and elsewhere) require language and cultural skills. New advisors should also come in with a thorough understanding of coalition force structure and the host nation's governing institutions. It is also critical that advisors learn how to advise. As one advisor workshop concluded, "Without training, advisors learned their jobs through trial and error, or failed completely. Training was needed to shorten the learning curve in order to prevent advisors from making not only 'rookie mistakes' but also

---

[1] Interviews with GCPSU SOAG staff, Kabul, Afghanistan, October 4 and 5, 2013.

[2] Numerous studies from Vietnam to the present day note that lack of training for advisory duties is a critical gap in U.S. capacity-building efforts. Many of these studies also note that better processes need to be in place to effectively select advisors for overseas missions: Brennan Cook, *Improving Security Force Assistance Capability in the Army's Advise and Assist Brigade*, School of Advanced Military Studies, 2010; Joint and Coalition Operational Analysis (JCOA), *Decade of War, Volume 1: Enduring Lessons from the Past Decade of Operations*, June 15, 2012; Carl Forsling, "Giving Advising Its Due," *Small Wars Journal*, January 22, 2014; Christopher Phelps, "Selecting and Training U.S. Advisors: Interpersonal Skills and the Advisor-Counterpart Relationship," master's thesis, University of Kansas, 2009; Thomas Clinton, *Lessons Learned from Advising and Training the Republic of South Vietnam's Armed Forces*, Ft. Leavenworth, Kan., 2007; Robert C. Muse, *Advising Foreign Forces: Force Structure Implications of the Indirect Approach to Irregular Warfare*, U.S. Marine Corps, Command and Staff College, 2008; Todd Clark, *Selection of Military Advisors*, Monterey, Calif.: Naval Postgraduate School, 2007.

irreparable errors."[3] Consequently, advisors should be trained in the art of influence and should understand both military and commercial industry best practices for advising and coaching.

Various pre-deployment training programs exist for officers working in the SOAGs. SOJTF-Bragg (SOJTF-B) is a command based in Ft. Bragg that consists of officers who are scheduled to deploy and serve in the Kabul-based SOJTF-A. This command, along with NATO Special Operations Headquarters (NSHQ), provides one- to two-week training seminars. The NATO SOF Training and Education Program, at the time of this research, provided a ten-day pre-deployment course for NATO personnel deploying to NSOCC-A and ISAF SOF. This training program provided a substantive review of NSOCC-A C2 structure and command processes (including individual briefings on subordinate elements), key SOF lines of effort, and threat networks. The course also includes a three-hour lecture on Afghan culture.[4] SOJTF-B provided a series of training opportunities, including a variety of leader professional development discussions, rehearsal of concept drills, and ongoing language familiarization classes. It also hosted a monthly five-day orientation seminar that provides an introduction to the NSOCC-A/SOJTF-A command mission and coalition and Afghan force structure. The seminar also includes a day of training designed to provide insight into Afghan culture, history, customs, and religion.[5] In addition, U.S. Special Operations Command hosts a one-week SOF Academic Week, which is heavily focused on current SOF operations in Afghanistan and in-theater SOF C2 architecture.

---

[3]   Victoria Stattel and Robert Perito, *Innovative Transformation: An Evaluation of the Ministry of Defense Advisors Program in Afghanistan*, Washington, D.C.: United States Institute of Peace, February 2012, p. 9.

[4]   NATO SOF Training and Education Program, *NSOCC-A and ISAF SOF Pre-Deployment Training Student Manual*, November 2013.

[5]   The orientation seminar also includes discussions on several key aspects that are deemed important to SOF operations in Afghanistan, including LNO procedures, VTC etiquette, and written communications. As noted, this training is conducted monthly, but SOJTF-B also offers one- to two-day special training sessions for personnel who are not able to attend the five-day seminar. Email correspondence with George Copeland, SOJTF-B, December 2, 2013.

Among U.S. advisors, the AFPAK Hands and Ministry of Defense Advisors (MODAs) enter the SOAGs with the most robust training. The AFPAK Hands program is a Joint Staff initiative whose goal is to create a cadre of highly trained officers with four-year commitments to the Afghan problem set. Accordingly, AFPAK Hands participate in an extensive four-month course in culture and language training, with refresher training that precedes a planned second tour. The MODA program recruits civilian advisors for ministerial-level capacity-building assignments in Afghanistan. The program provides seven weeks of block training, with five weeks specifically dedicated to advisor training.[6] The course includes instruction in language and culture, as well as country familiarization. It distinguishes itself from other training programs via its heavy focus on advising skills that seek to build "functional experts" skilled in advising and capacity building. The program also provides role-playing exercises and a final evaluation exercise that simulate the advisory experience in Afghanistan.[7]

Unfortunately, most individuals assigned to SOAGs, and likely other advisory units as well, do not participate in these training programs. Only a select few of the individuals within the SOAGs are AFPAK Hands or MODAs. SOJTF-B training seems more common for NSOCC-A staff than for SOAGs. Reports also suggest that only a minority of U.S. and NATO personnel sign up for the NSHQ course.[8] Several factors likely underpin this. For the NSHQ course, it seems cost is a prohibitive factor, with some contributing countries reluctant to pay travel and accommodation costs.[9] For many others, the issue is time. This is particularly the case for individual augmentees (IAs), who

---

[6]   The training program also includes two additional weeks of training that addresses administrative requirements, battlefield medicine, and security training.

[7]   Stattel and Perito, 2012. Commenting on the training, one MODA advisor observed,

> You learn when to speak and not to, how to phrase questions [so] you don't tell them what to do. You learn you can lead them in the direction you want to go. But the number one thing [you learn is that] Afghanistan is their country, we here to help but they must come up with solutions. (Interviews with ALP SOAG staff, Kabul, Afghanistan, October 8, 2013)

[8]   Interview with NATO officer, Kabul, Afghanistan, November 30, 2013.

[9]   Interview with NATO officer, Kabul, Afghanistan, November 30, 2013.

make up a large portion of SOAG staff. Many IAs receive their deployment orders relatively late, with three weeks pre-deployment notification not uncommon.[10]

To better prepare future operational-level advisors, several recommendations apply. First, ensure that as many advisors as possible participate in structured pre-deployment training coursework. For IAs, this will require advance notification for deployments, so that individuals have the requisite time to attend formal training events. It will also require that deployment orders for advisors clearly articulate specific pre-deployment training requirements. Beyond this, relevant commands at the force provider level, such as SOJTF-B and NSHQ, should take a cue from the MODA training. Though a five-week training block may not be feasible, force providers should incorporate specific training for the advisor mission, with lectures on state-of-the-art coaching, mentoring, and influence techniques. Training should also make ample use of role-playing exercises for both cultural competency and advising to help ingrain classroom lessons learned.[11] Providing a modicum of language capabilities is also key.

In the long run, it would be good for the U.S. Department of Defense to craft a more systematic approach to advisory training. For example, the Joint and Coalition Operational Analysis, a division of the Joint Staff J7, in its report entitled *Decade of War, Volume 1*, recommends that the U.S. reestablish of a Military Assistance and Training Advisory (MATA) course that would capitalize "recent lessons learned and Special Forces expertise" derived from recent foreign internal defense and security force assistance operations.[12] The MATA was first established in 1962 at Ft. Bragg's U.S. Special Warfare Center. The

---

[10]   One staffer, for example, noted that he always had high expectations for pre-deployment preparation, anticipating coursework in counterinsurgency, culture, and language. "So having said that, in three weeks you are told you are going to Afghanistan, [going to go to the SMW SOAG], [you'll] find out more when you get here. There is no prep time to do any of that." Interview with SMW SOAG and ETT staff, Kabul, Afghanistan, October 28 to November 1, 2013.

[11]   It seems that role-playing exercises would be especially critical in helping trainees learn to apply instruction for complex social interactions.

[12]   Joint and Coalition Operational Analysis, 2012.

course, taught by recently deployed Army and Marine Corps advisors, was six weeks long and focused on training Vietnamese culture and language and advisor tactics. In addition, in 1970, the Marine Corps established its own, three-month-long, "Marine Advisors Course."[13] Georgetown scholar and former Special Forces officer David Maxwell agrees with the Joint and Coalition Operational Analysis recommendation and argues that the new MATA course could not only serve as a pre-deployment training course but could also be used to "build up a cadre" of trained advisors across the joint force who could then be called upon for advisory duties as operations require (see text box).[14]

In addition to effective pre-deployment training, field headquarters that oversee advisors, such as NSOCC-A, and the SOAGs themselves should actively enhance in-theater training and education opportunities. First, NSOCC-A and its individual SOAGs should host Officer Professional Development (OPD) seminars and other in-theater training events. Such is the approach at Camp Commando, where the SOAG routinely invites guest lecturers to speak on key topics. For example, the former J7 at NSOCC-A, COL (P) Christopher Burns, is a reserve officer who works as a corporate coach for UBS in his civilian life. In this capacity, he coaches UBS's top financial earners to improve performance and enhance teamwork. In a Camp Commando OPD session, COL (P) Burns briefed the ANASOC SOAG on performance coaching. The session seemed to have a dramatic impact, as several SOAG staff heralded the session as highly influential. Taking advantage of experts resident in-theater is one approach. Opening the OPD to a VTC format could further tap into a deep reserve of military and civilian experts.

Second, teams of advisors should routinely conduct peer-sharing exercises. In peer-sharing exercises, an individual SOAG staff would ideally gather on a weekly or bi-weekly basis. During the meetings, individual advisory staff would share and discuss key advisory goals and approaches and discuss how their counterpart or partner staff are responding to mentoring efforts. COL (P) Burns argues that such exer-

---

[13] Clinton, 2007.

[14] Interview with COL (Retired) David Maxwell, Washington, D.C., January 30, 2014.

Text Box 7.1. Selection of Advisors

"There is a common misperception across the international donor community that any soldier, police officer, or other expert can be an effective advisor with a certain level of cultural and language training. This is simply false."[1]

There is growing recognition that not every soldier, sailor, marine, or airman has the personality and social skills suited to the advisory mission. The Department of the Army's manual for security force assistance notes that advisors must be "patient and personable enough to work effectively with" host-nation counterparts and that they require personality traits that allow them to "adapt and thrive in a foreign culture." Several key personality traits include tolerance for ambiguity, open-mindedness, empathy, and a tolerance for differences.[2] In a similar vein, one interview respondent commented that advisors should be "willing to live indigenously, willing to learn language, incorporate directives that are outlined but skim on the borders of those."[3] Another argued about the need to find individuals who are "low-key" rather than "aggressive."[4] Unfortunately, identifying individuals with the right temperament for advising is extremely difficult. For one, many of the identified characteristics are at odds with a U.S. military institution that prides itself in Type A personalities and hard chargers.[5] More significantly, there is no way to select for such personality traits when requesting forces through the Worldwide Individual Augmentee System (WIAS).

One remedy to this problem may lie in this chapter's recommendation to reinstitute the MATA course. For one, the course is a means to better train advisory skills in personnel throughout the uniformed services. More pertinently, the course could provide a means to identify able and willing advisors. First, personnel choosing to attend the course would likely be those with an affinity for the advisory mission. Second, performance ratings from the course could be added as an additional skill identifier for the WIAS and so enable commanders the opportunity to choose advisors with requisite skills.

---

[1] Nicholas Armstrong, "Afghanistan 2014–2024: Advising for Sustainability," *Small Wars Journal*, May 4, 2012.

[2] Headquarters, Department of the Army, 2009, p. 7-3

[3] Interviews with SMW SOAG and ETT staff, Kabul, Afghanistan, October 28 to November 1, 2013.

[4] Interviews with GCPSU SOAG staff, Kabul, Afghanista, October 4 and 5, 2013.

[5] Interview with COL (Retired) David Maxwell, Washington, D.C., January 30, 2014.

cises are routinely practiced at UBS, where he and a team of career coaches would meet to discuss individual cases and coaching techniques. The benefit of such an approach is that it provides a routine mechanism for information sharing, allows team members to learn from the tactics practiced by colleagues, and provides opportunity for SOAG directors to oversee SOAG advisory practices.

Summary

In summary, advisors need training in a variety of key areas, including language and cultural skills, coalition force structure and the host nation's governing institutions, C2, and logistics processes. Advisors should also learn how to advise. Relevant field commands, such as NSOCC-A, should create a block training event that addresses these key training requirements. Commanders should promote in-theater training and education opportunities and promote the use of advisor peer-sharing events. To more thoroughly inculcate advisory skills within the U.S. military, DoD should reinstitute the six-week Vietnam-era MATA course.

CHAPTER EIGHT

Continuity of Operations

> "Successive advisors to a single counterpart, having no record of past experience, face a long exploratory period in the advisory role. They are apt to repeat their predecessors' mistakes both in the psychological approach to the counterpart and in specific suggestions that may already have proved impracticable."[1]

It is critical that field commanders and advisory group directors develop manning policies and standard operating procedures that ensure that new and incoming advisors build on established relationships with host-nation partners, understand and apply previous lessons learned, and avoid unnecessary "reinventions of the wheel." The constant churn of incoming and outgoing staff within any deployed environment, including advisory commands, however, makes continuity an ever-present challenge.[2] The following recommended practices are drawn from the SOAGs and specific to the operational advisory mission.

Increase Tour Lengths for Key Advisory Positions

Tour lengths were a critical challenge to SOAG advisor efforts. Tour lengths of SOAG staffers varied considerably, from four to 12 months duration. U.S. marines and airmen, as well as many NATO personnel, typically served six-month tours. As previously noted, it reportedly

---

[1] Hickey, 1965.

[2] For a more in-depth review of continuity practices, see Todd C. Helmus and Austin Long, *Beyond the High Five: Managing Relief in Place at the Tactical and Operational Level*, Santa Monica, Calif.: RAND Corporation, 2013, not available to the general public.

takes one to three months for advisors to establish trusting relationships with their counterparts, which significantly cuts into a shortened tour. The problem is compounded by a reported "mentor fatigue," whereby Afghans tire of the revolving door of advisors.[3] Longer tours, in the realm of nine to 12 months, could help alleviate this problem. At a minimum, it may be wise to ensure that staff for key advisory positions (such as the director, J2, J3, and J4) serve yearlong tours.

Give Advance Notice on Deployments

Advance notification for deployments allows individuals an opportunity to prepare for deployment and enables them to connect in advance (via phone, email, and VTC) with those they are to replace. At the time of this study, most SOAG staffers were IAs, and it appears that three-weeks' notice for an impending deployment was not uncommon. Others reported frequent and last-minute changes in their assignment, thus nullifying portions of their pre-deployment training. For example, a British officer at GCPSU SOAG commented that he prepared for a deployment to Helmand Province only to find late that he was to serve a SOAG mission.[4] According to an ANASOC SOAG staffer: "I deployed by myself, I was told three different locations. [First Camp Integrity, second Camp Eggers] and then while at Ft. Benning they said just kidding, come to Camp Morehead [instead]. . . . No one knew what Camp Morehead was, I never heard of it."[5] Ultimately, securing advance notification for IAs requires careful and long-range planning. Request for Forces memoranda must be submitted at least six months out or more to give the request time to circulate through appropriate approval channels and allow the identification of willing candidates. Once individuals are identified, it is important to notify them of their impending assignment. Last-minute changes in assignments should be avoided where possible.

---

[3]   Interviews with GCPSU SOAG staff, Kabul, Afghanistan, October 4 and 5, 2013.

[4]   Interviews with GCPSU SOAG staff, Kabul, Afghanistan, October 4 and 5, 2013.

[5]   Interviews with ANASOC SOAG staff, Kabul, Afghanistan, October 8 and 9, 2013.

Ensure Proper Relief in Place/Transfer of Authority (RIP/TOA) Periods

Continuity requires proper periods of overlap between incoming and outgoing personnel to enable right-seat/left-seat transitions and to allow effective transfer of information. Though not necessarily the norm, several advisors identified sorely abbreviated RIP lengths or gaps in assignments that left no opportunity for a relief in place. In one case, the incoming ANASOC SOAG met their counterparts at the airport, where they received the proverbial "high five."[6] Meanwhile numerous RIP gaps were reported at the SMW, where there was a two-month gap between outgoing and incoming commanders and a three-month gap for the executive officer.[7] Sporadic gaps among staff were reported for other SOAG positions as well.

Properly Organize and Maintain Computer Portals

Computer portals represent a constant continuity challenge. The ability to easily find, search, and retrieve relevant documents, including situation reports, operational orders, plans, KLE summaries, etc., aids continuity by allowing new arrivals (and those preparing for deployment) to get up to speed and prevents duplication of planning efforts. The challenge is that maintaining proper portals is a cumbersome task, and, without command guidance, many staffers revert to the default of storing key files on computer hard drives. Providing a best practice, ALP SOAG has made a conscious effort to manage its CENTRIX portal. The group tasked a noncommissioned officer to clean and organize the portal, including removing duplicate items and organizing files by topic. At the time of this research, it was policy for staff to place all new documents in the portal with proper date and naming conventions. Now, new and incoming staff receive a link to the portal and

---

[6] Interviews with ANASOC SOAG staff, Kabul, Afghanistan, October 8 and 9, 2013.

[7] Interviews with SMW SOAG and ETT staff, Kabul, Afghanistan, October 28 to November 1, 2013.

are urged to work their way through the documents. Such a practice should be replicated across the SOAGs. Like the ALP SOAG, it will be necessary to identify an information management officer, who must not only organize existing portals but also enforce data management practices across the advisory group or command.

Prepare a Continuity Book

A related approach to information management is to create continuity folders. One staffer at Commando SOAG wrote a continuity paper that sought to educate his replacement on the history of his advisory efforts, the organization of his Afghan unit, key challenges, and his outlined way ahead.[8] Alternatively, the SMW ETT executive officer required all the individuals he rated to keep and update a working continuity book. These books include relevant organizational charts, phone rosters, training schedules, relevant MI-17 manuals, and a narrative description of key programmatic efforts and challenges.[9] Such books complement SharePoint computer files because they provide an easy and quick reference guide and importantly help tell a narrative story of what are often complex advisory efforts.[10] Such continuity books should be a requirement of all key staff positions.

Harness Experienced Staff

Most SOAGs employ a "trickle" approach to staffing, whereby staff rotate in and out on individual levels. One benefit of this trickle approach is that although someone new is always on the staff, there is also someone who has been in place for some time and can maintain continuity. Different SOAGs approached this type of continuity

---

[8]   Interviews with ANASOC SOAG staff, Kabul, Afghanistan, October 8 and 9, 2013.

[9]   Interview with SMW SOAG and ETT staff, Kabul, Afghanistan, October 28 to November 1, 2013.

[10]   Interviews with ANASOC SOAG staff, Kabul, Afghanistan, October 8 and 9, 2013.

in different ways. At base, it meant that everyone who has been on staff for several months or more has responsibility to train and advise the newcomers. Such was the approach at SMW, where the close-knit staff were already gearing up to help a newcomer whose arrival date precluded an adequate RIP.[11] Alternatively, GCPSU SOAG assigned one of their long-term staffers to play the role of "Mr. Continuity." Mr. Continuity worked to educate incoming staff members on SOAG policies and lines of effort, answer key questions, and help identify critical SOAG documents.[12] Of course, commanders have ultimate responsibility for continuity.

Standardize Pre-Deployment Training

The content and extent of pre-deployment training can influence the character of advising. Significant variations in such training across individual rotations are therefore likely to affect continuity of mentee relationships as well as other advisory practices. Some individuals begin the advisory mission with language, culture, and advisory training, whereas others do not. Some will take an indirect, questions-based approach to advising, while others may take a more directive, tell-them-how-to-do-it approach. To the extent that advisory commands can help develop a more standardized pre-deployment training package for incoming staff, variation in mentorship approaches will be reduced.

Summary

Increased tour lengths, advance deployment notifications, sufficiently long RIP/TOA lengths, proper share drive storage, continuity books, and even standardized pre-deployment training packages are all steps that advisory groups can undertake to enhance continuity across

---

[11] Interviews with SMW SOAG and ETT staff, Kabul, Afghanistan, October 28 to November 1, 2013.

[12] Interviews with ANASOC SOAG staff, Kabul, Afghanistan, October 8 and 9, 2013.

incoming and outgoing advisors. To ensure that individual advisory groups consistently apply these practices, NSOCC-A and other relevant commands should issue formal continuity guidelines to subordinate elements.

CHAPTER NINE

Conclusion

This report draws from the experiences of NSOCC-A SOAGs to identify best practices for building partner capacity at the operational headquarters level. Advisors should assiduously seek to build rapport with host-nation counterparts and apply the nuanced art of advising counterparts in ways that cultivate problem-solving skills and ownership of solutions. Advisors should carefully cultivate relationships across the network of coalition mentors and help partners build such connections across the host nation's security architecture. Enhancing partner sustainability is a critically important goal and can be accomplished in part by simplifying host-nation operations and procurement requirements, building effective unit processes, and weaning partner forces from coalition enablers. To most effectively carry out the advisor mission, the United States and its allies, including NATO, should prepare advisors for the mission at hand with training that not only builds language and cultural skills but also gives prospective advisors the necessary tools for advising. Continuity of operations is especially critical and will require effective manning policies, as well as command guidance on key continuity standard operating procedures.

Of course, the content in this report draws from only a small piece of the SOAG mission. Each SOAG is unique and encompasses a host of programmatic and capacity-building initiatives that are beyond the scope of this report. Furthermore, each individual section of this report touches only the surface of relevant best practices. It will ultimately fall on U.S. and NATO forces to build effective pre-deployment training coursework to present a more comprehensive picture of the SOAG and related advisory missions.

Abbreviations

ABP	Afghan Border Police
AfPak	Afghanistan-Pakistan
ALP	Afghan Local Police
ANA	Afghan National Army
ANASF	ANA Special Forces
ANASOC	Afghan National Army Special Operations Command
ANSF	Afghan National Security Forces
ANTS	Afghan National Tracking System
ASSF	Afghan Special Security Forces
C2	command and control
CF	Commando Force
CRU	Crisis Response Unit
ETT	Embedded Training Team
GCPSU	General Command of Police Special Units
IA	individual augmentee
ISAF	International Security Assistance Force
ISR	intelligence, surveillance, and reconnaissance
KLE	key leader engagement
LNO	liaison officer
MAG SOFLE	Ministry Advisory Group Special Operations Forces Liaison Element

MATA	Military Assistance and Training Advisory
MOD	Ministry of Defense
MODA	Ministry of Defense Advisors
MOI	Ministry of Interior
NDS	National Directorate of Security
NMIC	National Military Intelligence Center
NMU	National Mission Units
NSHQ	NATO Special Operations Headquarters
NSOCC-A	NATO Special Operations Component Command–Afghanistan
NTEC	National Targeting Exploitation Center
O&I	operations and intelligence
OPD	Officer Professional Development
PSU	Provincial Special Unit
RIP/TOA	relief in place/transfer of authority
SIU	Special Investigative Units
SMW	Special Mission Wing
SNCO	senior noncommissioned officer
SOAG	Special Operations Advisory Group
SOB	special operations brigade
SOF	Special Operations Forces
SOJTF-A	Special Operations Joint Task Force–Afghanistan
SOJTF-B	Special Operations Joint Task Force–Bragg
SOK	special operations kandak
TOC	tactical operations center
UNAMA	United Nations Assistance Mission Afghanistan
VSO	Village Stability Operations
VTC	video teleconference

Bibliography

Armstrong, Nicholas, "Afghanistan 2014–2024: Advising for Sustainability," *Small Wars Journal*, May 4, 2012.

Brounstein, Marty, *Coaching and Mentoring for Dummies: A Reference for the Rest of Us*, Hoboken, N.J.: Wiley Publishing, Inc., 2000.

Campbell, Jason, Matthew Thomeczek and Todd C. Helmus, "Best Practices for Building SOF Partnership Capacity—Intelligence Highlights," NSOCC-A Commander's Initiative Group paper, September 24, 2013.

Clark, Todd, *Selection of Military Advisors*, Monterrey, Calif.: Naval Postgraduate School, 2007.

Clinton, Thomas, *Lessons Learned from Advising and Training the Republic of South Vietnam's Armed Forces*, Ft. Leavenworth, Kan., 2007.

Cook, Brennan, *Improving Security Force Assistance Capability in the Army's Advise and Assist Brigade*, School of Advanced Military Studies, 2010.

Forsling, Carl, "Giving Advising Its Due," *Small Wars Journal*, January 22, 2014.

Headquarters, Department of the Army, *Security Force Assistance*, Field Manual 3-07.1, May 2009.

Helmus, Todd C., and Austin Long, *Beyond the High Five: Managing Relief in Place at the Tactical and Operational Level*, Santa Monica, Calif.: RAND Corporation, 2013, not available to the general public.

Hickey, Gerald Cannon, *The American Military Advisor and His Foreign Counterpart: The Case of Vietnam,* Santa Monica, Calif.: RAND Corporation, RM-4482-ARPA, 1965. As of February 4, 2015: http://www.rand.org/pubs/research_memoranda/RM4482.html

Joint and Coalition Operational Analysis, *Decade of War, Volume 1: Enduring Lessons from the Past Decade of Operations*, June 15, 2012.

Long, Austin, Todd C. Helmus, S. Rebecca Zimmerman, Christopher M. Schnaubelt, and Peter Chalk, *Building Special Operations Partnerships in Afghanistan and Beyond: Challenges and Best Practices from Afghanistan, Iraq, and Colombia*, Santa Monica, Calif.: RAND Corporation, forthcoming.

Maister, David H., Charles H. Green, and Robert M. Galford, *The Trusted Advisor*, New York: The Free Press, 2000.

Marquis, Jefferson, Jennifer D. P. Moroney, Justin Beck, Derek Eaton, Scott Hiromoto, David R. Howell, Janet Lewis, Charlotte Lynch, Michael J. Neumann, and Cathryn Quantic Thurston, *Developing an Army Strategy for Building Partner Capacity for Stability Operations*, Santa Monica, Calif.: RAND Corporation, MG-942-A, 2010. As of February 4, 2015:
http://www.rand.org/pubs/monographs/MG942.html

Moroney, Jennifer D. P., Adam Grissom, and Jefferson P. Marquis, *A Capabilities-Based Strategy for Army Security Cooperation*, Santa Monica, Calif.: RAND Corporation, MG-563-A, 2007. As of February 4, 2015:
http://www.rand.org/pubs/monographs/MG563.html

Moroney, Jennifer D. P., Celeste Gventer, Stephanie Pezard, and Laurence Smallman, *Lessons from U.S. Allies in Security Cooperation with Third Countries: The Cases of Australia, France, and the United Kingdom*, Santa Monica, Calif.: RAND Corporation, TR-972-AF, 2011. As of February 4, 2015:
http://www.rand.org/pubs/technical_reports/TR972.html

Muse, Robert C., *Advising Foreign Forces: Force Structure Implications of the Indirect Approach to Irregular Warfare*, United States Marine Corps, Command and Staff College, 2008.

NATO SOF Training and Education Program, *NSOCC-A and ISAF SOF Pre-Deployment Training Student Manual*, November 2013.

Paul, Christopher, Colin P. Clarke, Beth Grill, Stephanie Young, Jennifer D. P. Moroney, Joe Hogler, and Christine Leah, *What Works Best in Building Partner Capacity and Under What Circumstances?* Santa Monica, Calif.: RAND Corporation, MG-1253/1-OSD, 2013. As of February 4, 2015:
http://www.rand.org/pubs/monographs/MG1253z1.html

Payne, Leslie Adrienne, and Jan Osburg, *Leveraging Observations of Security Force Assistance in Afghanistan for Global Operations*, Santa Monica, Calif.: RAND Corporation, RR-416-A, 2013. As of February 4, 2015:
http://www.rand.org/pubs/research_reports/RR416.html

Phelps, Christopher, "Selecting and Training U.S. Advisors: Interpersonal Skills and the Advisor-Counterpart Relationship," master's thesis, University of Kansas, 2009.

Ramsey III, Robert D., "Advising Indigenous Forces: American Advisors in Korea, Vietnam, and El Salvador," *Global War on Terrorism Occasional Paper 18*, Fort Leavenworth, Kan.: Combat Studies Institute Press, 2006.

Stattel, Victoria, and Robert Perito, *Innovative Transformation: An Evaluation of the Ministry of Defense Advisors Program in Afghanistan*, Washington, D.C.: United States Institute of Peace, February 2012.